D1447146

To:

_____

From:

_____

Date:

_____

# Psalms

## FOR
## JOYFUL LIVING

CHRISTIAN ART
PUBLISHERS

*Psalms for Joyful Living*

© 2003 Christian Art Publishers
PO Box 1599, Vereeniging, 1930, RSA

First edition 2003
Second edition 2012
Third edition 2020

Designed by Christian Art Publishers
Cover designed by Christian Art Publishers

Images used under license from Shutterstock.com

Scripture quotations are taken from the *Holy Bible*,
English Standard Version®. Copyright © 2001 by Crossway, a
publishing ministry of Good News Publishers.
Used by permission. All rights reserved.

Scripture quotations are taken from the *Holy Bible*,
King James Version, and are in the public domain.

Scripture quotations are taken from the New King James
Version®. Copyright © 1982 by Thomas Nelson.
Used by permission. All rights reserved.

Scripture quotations are taken from the *Holy Bible*, New
International Version®, NIV® Copyright © 1973, 1978, 1984,
2011 by Biblica, Inc.® Used by permission.
All rights reserved worldwide.

Printed in China

ISBN 978-1-4321-3273-6

23  24  25  26  27  28  29  30  31  32  -  11  10  9  8  7  6  5  4  3  2

# Contents

# ANGER

O LORD, rebuke me not in Your anger, nor discipline me in Your wrath.

Psalm 6:1 (ESV)

Arise, O LORD, in Your anger; lift Yourself up because of the rage of my enemies; rise up for me to the judgment You have commanded!

Psalm 7:6 (NKJV)

Then the earth reeled and rocked; the foundations also of the mountains trembled and quaked, because He was angry.

Psalm 18:7 (ESV)

At Your rebuke, O God of Jacob, both horse and chariot lie still. You alone are to be feared. Who can stand before You when You are angry?

Psalm 76:6-7 (NIV)

# ANGER

For they provoked Him to anger with their high places; they moved Him to jealousy with their idols.

Psalm 78:58 (ESV)

Yet He was merciful; He forgave their iniquities and did not destroy them. Time after time He restrained His anger and did not stir up His full wrath.

Psalm 78:38 (NIV)

Who knows the power of Your anger? For as the fear of You, so is Your wrath.

Psalm 90:11 (NKJV)

The LORD is merciful and gracious, slow to anger and abounding in steadfast love. He will not always chide, nor will He keep His anger forever.

Psalm 103:8-9 (ESV)

# BLESSING

Blessed is the man that walketh not in the counsel of the ungodly, nor standeth in the way of sinners, nor sitteth in the seat of the scornful. But his delight is in the law of the Lord; and in His law doth he meditate day and night.

Psalm 1:1-2 (KJV)

For You bless the righteous, O Lord; You cover him with favor as with a shield.

Psalm 5:12 (ESV)

He will receive blessing from the Lord and vindication from God his Savior. Such is the generation of those who seek Him.

Psalm 24:5-6 (NIV)

The Lord will give strength to His people; the Lord will bless His people with peace.

Psalm 29:11 (NKJV)

# BLESSING

Blessed is he whose transgressions are forgiven, whose sins are covered. Blessed is the man whose sin the LORD does not count against him and in whose spirit is no deceit.

Psalm 32:1-2 (NIV)

Blessed is he that considereth the poor: the LORD will deliver him in time of trouble.

Psalm 41:1 (KJV)

May the peoples praise You, O God; may all the peoples praise You. Then the land will yield its harvest, and God, our God, will bless us. God will bless us, and all the ends of the earth will fear Him.

Psalm 67:5-7 (NIV)

Blessed is the man whose strength is in You, whose heart is set on pilgrimage.

Psalm 84:5 (NKJV)

# BLESSING

Oh, that men would give thanks to the LORD for His goodness, and for His wonderful works to the children of men! He also blesses them, and they multiply greatly; and He does not let their cattle decrease.

Psalm 107:31, 38 (NKJV)

Praise the LORD! Blessed is the man who fears the LORD, who greatly delights in His commandments!

Psalm 112:1 (ESV)

The LORD remembers us and will bless us: He will bless the house of Israel, He will bless the house of Aaron, He will bless those who fear the LORD – small and great alike. May the LORD make you increase, both you and your children. May you be blessed by the LORD, the Maker of heaven and earth.

Psalm 115:12-15 (NIV)

# BLESSING

Blessed is he who comes in the name of the LORD! We bless you from the house of the LORD.

Psalm 118:26 (ESV)

Blessed are the undefiled in the way, who walk in the law of the LORD. Blessed are they that keep His testimonies, and that seek Him with the whole heart.

Psalm 119:1-2 (KJV)

Blessed is everyone who fears the LORD, who walks in His ways! You shall eat the fruit of the labor of your hands; you shall be blessed, and it shall be well with you.

Psalm 128:1-2 (ESV)

The LORD bless you from Zion! May you see the prosperity of Jerusalem all the days of your life! May you see your children's children! Peace be upon Israel!

Psalm 128:5-6 (ESV)

# Confession

I acknowledged my sin unto Thee, and mine iniquity have I not hid. I said, I will confess my transgressions unto the LORD; and Thou forgavest the iniquity of my sin.

Psalm 32:5 (KJV)

Have mercy upon me, O God, according to Your lovingkindness; according to the multitude of Your tender mercies, blot out my transgressions. Wash me thoroughly from my iniquity, and cleanse me from my sin. Against You, You only, have I sinned, and done this evil in Your sight – that You may be found just when You speak, and blameless when You judge. Purge me with hyssop, and I shall be clean; wash me, and I shall be whiter than snow. Hide Your face from my sins, and blot out all my iniquities. Create in me a clean heart, O God, and renew a steadfast spirit within me.

Psalm 51:1-2, 4, 7, 9-10 (NKJV)

# Confession

Because of Your wrath there is no health in my body; my bones have no soundness because of my sin. My guilt has overwhelmed me like a burden too heavy to bear. I confess my iniquity; I am troubled by my sin.

Psalm 38:3- 4, 18 (NIV)

As for me, I said, "O LORD, be gracious to me; heal me, for I have sinned against You!" But You, O LORD, be gracious to me, and raise me up, that I may repay them!

Psalm 41:4, 10 (ESV)

O God, Thou knowest my foolishness; and my sins are not hid from Thee.

Psalm 69:5 (KJV)

Both we and our fathers have sinned; we have committed iniquity; we have done wickedness.

Psalm 106:6 (ESV)

# DISTRESS

Answer me, O LORD, out of the goodness of Your love; in Your great mercy turn to me. Do not hide Your face from Your servant; answer me quickly, for I am in trouble. Come near and rescue me.

Psalm 69:16-18 (NIV)

When I was in distress, I sought the Lord; at night I stretched out untiring hands and my soul refused to be comforted. Then I thought, "To this I will appeal: the years of the right hand of the Most High." I will remember the deeds of the LORD; yes, I will remember Your miracles of long ago.

Psalm 77:2, 10-11 (NIV)

Thou calledst in trouble, and I delivered thee; I answered thee in the secret place of thunder: I proved thee at the waters of Meribah.

Psalm 81:7 (KJV)

# DISTRESS

When anxiety was great within me, Your consolation brought joy to my soul.

Psalm 94:19 (NKJV)

Do not hide Your face from me in the day of my distress! Incline Your ear to me; answer me speedily in the day when I call!

Psalm 102:2 (ESV)

They fell down, and there was none to help. Then they cried out to the LORD in their trouble, and He saved them out of their distresses. He brought them out of darkness and the shadow of death, and broke their chains in pieces.

Psalm 107:12-14 (NKJV)

Give us help from trouble: for vain is the help of man.

Psalm 108:12 (KJV)

# DISTRESS

The sorrows of death compassed me, and the pains of hell gat hold upon me: I found trouble and sorrow. Then called I upon the name of the LORD; O LORD, I beseech Thee, deliver my soul.

Psalm 116:3-4 (KJV)

Trouble and anguish have overtaken me, yet Your commandments are my delights.

Psalm 119:143 (NKJV)

Though I walk in the midst of trouble, You preserve my life; You stretch out Your hand against the anger of my foes, with Your right hand You save me. The LORD will fulfill His purpose for me; Your love, O LORD, endures forever.

Psalm 138:7-8 (NIV)

I pour out my complaint before Him; I declare before Him my trouble.

Psalm 142:2 (NKJV)

# Eternal life

The Lord is King for ever and ever; the nations will perish from His land.

Psalm 10:16 (NIV)

But I have trusted in Thy mercy; my heart shall rejoice in Thy salvation.

Psalm 13:5 (KJV)

Therefore my heart is glad, and my whole being rejoices; my flesh also dwells secure. For You will not abandon my soul to Sheol, or let Your holy one see corruption.

Psalm 16:9-10 (ESV)

The Lord is my rock and my fortress and my deliverer, my God, my rock, in whom I take refuge, my shield, and the horn of my salvation, my stronghold.

Psalm 18:2 (ESV)

# ETERNAL LIFE

Thou hast also given me the shield of Thy salvation: and Thy right hand hath holden me up, and Thy gentleness hath made me great.

Psalm 18:35 (KJV)


Surely goodness and mercy shall follow me all the days of my life: and I will dwell in the house of the LORD for ever.

Psalm 23:6 (KJV)


For with You is the fountain of life; in Your light do we see light.

Psalm 36:9 (ESV)


Truly my soul waiteth upon God: from Him cometh my salvation. He only is my rock and my salvation; He is my defence; I shall not be greatly moved.

Psalm 62:1-2 (KJV)

# ETERNAL LIFE

For God is my King of old, working salvation in the midst of the earth.

Psalm 74:12 (KJV)

Surely His salvation is near to those who fear Him, that glory may dwell in our land.

Psalm 85:9 (ESV)

Be exalted, O God, above the heavens, and Your glory above all the earth; that Your beloved may be delivered, save with Your right hand, and hear me.

Psalm 108:5-6 (NKJV)

For the LORD taketh pleasure in His people: He will beautify the meek with salvation.

Psalm 149:4 (KJV)

# FAITHFULNESS

The LORD has dealt with me according to my righteousness; according to the cleanness of my hands He has rewarded me. For I have kept the ways of the LORD; I have not done evil by turning from my God.

Psalm 18:20-21 (NIV)

All the paths of the LORD are mercy and truth, to such as keep His covenant and His testimonies.

Psalm 25:10 (NKJV)

Love the LORD, all you His saints! The LORD preserves the faithful but abundantly repays the one who acts in pride.

Psalm 31:23 (ESV)

For the LORD loveth judgment, and forsaketh not His saints; they are preserved for ever: but the seed of the wicked shall be cut off.

Psalm 37:28 (KJV)

# FAITHFULNESS

I desire to do Your will, O my God; Your law is within my heart.

Psalm 40:8 (ESV)

Consider this, you who forget God, or I will tear you to pieces, with none to rescue: He who sacrifices thank offerings honors me, and He prepares the way so that I may show Him the salvation of God.

Psalm 50:22-23 (NIV)

You who love the LORD, hate evil! He preserves the souls of His saints; He delivers them out of the hand of the wicked.

Psalm 97:10 (NKJV)

My eyes shall be on the faithful of the land, that they may dwell with me; he who walks in a perfect way, he shall serve me.

Psalm 101:6 (NKJV)

# FAITHFULNESS

But from everlasting to everlasting the LORD's love
is with those who fear Him, and His righteousness
with their children's children – with those who keep
His covenant and remember to obey His precepts.

Psalm 103:17-18 (NIV)

I understand more than the ancients, because I keep
Thy precepts. I have refrained my feet from every evil
way, that I might keep Thy word.

Psalm 119:100-101 (KJV)

If your sons keep My covenant and My testimonies
that I shall teach them, their sons also forever shall
sit on your throne.

Psalm 132:12 (ESV)

Surely the righteous shall give thanks to Your name;
the upright shall dwell in Your presence.

Psalm 140:13 (ESV)

# FAMILY

But You do see, for You note mischief and vexation, that you may take it into Your hands; to You the helpless commits himself; You have been the helper of the fatherless.

Psalm 10:14 (ESV)

You still the hunger of those You cherish; their sons have plenty, and they store up wealth for their children.

Psalm 17:14 (NIV)

When my father and my mother forsake me, then the LORD will take me up.

Psalm 27:10 (KJV)

I have been young, and now am old; yet I have not seen the righteous forsaken, nor His descendants begging bread. He is ever merciful, and lends; and His descendants are blessed.

Psalm 37:25-26 (NKJV)

# FAMILY

We have heard with our ears, O God, our fathers have told us, what work Thou didst in their days, in the times of old.

Psalm 44:1 (KJV)

I will open my mouth in a parable; I will utter dark sayings from of old, things that we have heard and known, that our fathers have told us. We will not hide them from their children, but tell to the coming generation the glorious deeds of the LORD, and His might.

Psalm 78:2-4 (ESV)

As a father has compassion on his children, so the LORD has compassion on those who fear Him.

Psalm 103:13 (NIV)

He gives the barren woman a home, making her the joyous mother of children.

Psalm 113:9 (ESV)

# FAMILY

But the mercy of the LORD is from everlasting to everlasting upon them that fear Him, and His righteousness unto children's children; to such as keep His covenant, and to those that remember His commandments to do them.

Psalm 103:17-18 (KJV)

May the LORD give you increase, you and your children! May you be blessed by the LORD, who made heaven and earth! The heavens are the LORD's heavens, but the earth He has given to the children of man.

Psalm 115:14-16 (ESV)

Behold, children are a heritage from the LORD, the fruit of the womb is a reward. Like arrows in the hand of a warrior, so are the children of one's youth. Happy is the man who has his quiver full of them.

Psalm 127:3-5 (NKJV)

# FAMILY

Your wife shall be like a fruitful vine in the very heart of your house, your children like olive plants all around your table.

Psalm 128:3 (NKJV)

Surely I have calmed and quieted my soul, like a weaned child with his mother; like a weaned child is my soul within me.

Psalm 131:1-2 (NKJV)

Then our sons in their youth will be like well-nurtured plants, and our daughters will be like pillars carved to adorn a palace.

Psalm 144:12 (NIV)

One generation shall commend Your works to another, and shall declare Your mighty acts.

Psalm 145:4 (ESV)

Praise the LORD from the earth … both young men, and maidens; old men, and children.

Psalm 148:7, 12 (KJV)

# FEAR

I will not be afraid of ten thousands of people, that have set themselves against me round about.

Psalm 3:6 (KJV)

The cords of death entangled me; the torrents of destruction overwhelmed me. The cords of the grave coiled around me; the snares of death confronted me. In my distress I called to the LORD; I cried to my God for help. From His temple He heard my voice; my cry came before Him, into His ears.

Psalm 18:4-6 (NIV)

He restoreth my soul: He leadeth me in the paths of righteousness for His name's sake. Yea, though I walk through the valley of the shadow of death, I will fear no evil: for Thou art with me; Thy rod and Thy staff they comfort me.

Psalm 23:3-4 (KJV)

# FEAR

The LORD is my light and my salvation – whom shall I fear? The LORD is the stronghold of my life – of whom shall I be afraid? When evil men advance against me to devour my flesh, when my enemies and my foes attack me, they will stumble and fall. Though an army besiege me, my heart will not fear; though war break out against me, even then will I be confident.

Psalm 27:1-3 (NIV)

God is our refuge and strength, a very present help in trouble. Therefore we will not fear, even though the earth be removed, and though the mountains be carried into the midst of the sea; though its waters roar and be troubled, though the mountains shake with its swelling.

Psalm 46:1-3 (NKJV)

# FEAR

When I am afraid, I put my trust in You. In God, whose word I praise, in God I trust; I shall not be afraid. What can flesh do to me? In God I trust; I shall not be afraid. What can man do to me?

Psalm 56:3-4, 11 (ESV)

(He) made His own people to go forth like sheep, and guided them in the wilderness like a flock. He led them on safely, so that they feared not.

Psalm 78:52-53 (KJV)

He shall cover you with His feathers, and under His wings you shall take refuge; His truth shall be your shield and buckler. You shall not be afraid of the terror by night, nor of the arrow that flies by day, nor of the pestilence that walks in darkness, nor of the destruction that lays waste at noonday.

Psalm 91:4-6 (NKJV)

# FEAR

Surely he will never be shaken; a righteous man will be remembered forever. He will have no fear of bad news; his heart is steadfast, trusting in the LORD. His heart is secure, he will have no fear; in the end he will look in triumph on his foes.

Psalm 112:6-8 (NIV)

In my anguish I cried to the LORD, and He answered by setting me free. The LORD is with me; I will not be afraid. What can man do to me? The LORD is with me; he is my helper. I will look in triumph on my enemies.

Psalm 118:5-7 (NIV)

My flesh trembles for fear of You, and I am afraid of Your judgments.

Psalm 119:120 (NKJV)

# GOD'S FAITHFULNESS

Into Your hand I commit my spirit; You have redeemed me, O LORD, faithful God.

Psalm 31:5 (ESV)

Your steadfast love, O LORD, extends to the heavens, Your faithfulness to the clouds.

Psalm 36:5 (ESV)

Commit your way to the LORD, trust also in Him, and He shall bring it to pass.

Psalm 37:5 (NKJV)

I do not hide Your righteousness in my heart; I speak of Your faithfulness and salvation. I do not conceal Your love and Your truth from the great assembly.

Psalm 40:10 (NIV)

Shall Thy lovingkindness be declared in the grave or Thy faithfulness in destruction?

Psalm 88:11 (KJV)

# GOD'S FAITHFULNESS

I will sing of the steadfast love of the Lord, forever; with my mouth I will make known Your faithfulness to all generations. For I said, "Steadfast love will be built up forever; in the heavens You will establish Your faithfulness."

Psalm 89:1-2 (ESV)

And the heavens shall praise Thy wonders, O Lord: Thy faithfulness also in the congregation of the saints.

Psalm 89:5 (KJV)

It is good to give thanks to the Lord, and to sing praises to Your name, O Most High; to declare Your lovingkindness in the morning, and Your faithfulness every night.

Psalm 92:1-2 (NKJV)

# GOD'S FAITHFULNESS

For the LORD is good; His steadfast love endures forever, and His faithfulness to all generations.

Psalm 100:5 (ESV)

They are steadfast for ever and ever, done in faithfulness and uprightness.

Psalm 111:8 (NIV)

Your faithfulness endures to all generations; You established the earth, and it abides.

Psalm 119:90 (NKJV)

Thy testimonies that Thou hast commanded are righteous and very faithful.

Psalm 119:138 (KJV)

Your kingdom is an everlasting kingdom, and Your dominion endures throughout all generations.

Psalm 145:13 (ESV)

# GOD'S GLORY

The heavens declare the glory of God, and the sky above proclaims His handiwork.

Psalm 19:1 (ESV)

Ascribe to the LORD, O mighty ones, ascribe to the LORD glory and strength. Ascribe to the LORD the glory due His name; worship the LORD in the splendor of His holiness.

Psalm 29:1-2 (NIV)

Be exalted, O God, above the heavens; let Your glory be above all the earth.

Psalm 57:5 (NKJV)

So I have looked upon You in the sanctuary, beholding Your power and glory.

Psalm 63:2 (ESV)

And blessed be His glorious name forever! And let the whole earth be filled with His glory. Amen and Amen.

Psalm 72:19 (NKJV)

# God's glory

You are resplendent with light, more majestic than mountains rich with game.

Psalm 76:4 (NIV)

The LORD reigns, He is robed in majesty; the LORD is robed in majesty and is armed with strength.

Psalm 93:1 (NIV)

Be exalted, O God, above the heavens! Let Your glory be over all the earth!

Psalm 108:5 (ESV)

His work is honorable and glorious, and His righteousness endures forever.

Psalm 111:3 (NKJV)

I will meditate on the glorious splendor of Your majesty, and on Your wondrous works.

Psalm 145:5 (NKJV)

# GOD'S GREATNESS

O LORD, our Lord, how excellent is Your name in all the earth, who have set Your glory above the heavens! When I consider Your heavens, the work of Your fingers, the moon and the stars, which You have ordained, what is man that You are mindful of him, and the son of man that You visit him?

Psalm 8:1, 3-4 (NKJV)

The LORD is in His holy temple, the LORD's throne is in heaven: His eyes behold, His eyelids try the children of men.

Psalm 11:4 (KJV)

For who is God, but the LORD? And who is a rock, except our God? – the God who equipped me with strength and made my way blameless. He made my feet like the feet of a deer and set me secure on the heights.

Psalm 18:31-33 (ESV)

# GOD'S GREATNESS

By the word of the LORD the heavens were made,
and all the host of them by the breath of His mouth.

Psalm 33:6 (NKJV)

Your ways, O God, are holy. What god is so great as
our God? You are the God who performs miracles;
You display Your power among the peoples.

Psalm 77:13-14 (NIV)

The heavens are Thine, the earth also is Thine: as
for the world and the fulness thereof, Thou hast
founded them.

Psalm 89:11 (KJV)

He counts the number of the stars; He calls them all
by name. Great is our Lord, and mighty in power; His
understanding is infinite.

Psalm 147:4-5 (NKJV)

# GOD'S JUSTICE

Therefore the ungodly shall not stand in the judgment, nor sinners in the congregation of the righteous. For the LORD knows the way of the righteous, but the way of the ungodly shall perish.

Psalm 1:5-6 (NKJV)

The LORD shall judge the people: judge me, O LORD, according to my righteousness, and according to mine integrity that is in me. Oh let the wickedness of the wicked come to an end; but establish the just: for the righteous God trieth the hearts and reigns.

Psalm 7:8-9 (KJV)

God is a just judge, and God is angry with the wicked every day. If He does not turn back, He will sharpen His sword; He bends His bow and makes it ready.

Psalm 7:11-12 (NKJV)

# GOD'S JUSTICE

You have maintained my just cause; You have sat on the throne, giving righteous judgment.

Psalm 9:4 (ESV)

The LORD tests the righteous, but His soul hates the wicked and the one who loves violence. Let him rain coals on the wicked; fire and sulfur and a scorching wind shall be the portion of their cup. For the LORD is righteous; He loves righteous deeds; the upright shall behold His face.

Psalm 11:5-7 (ESV)

The law of the LORD is perfect, converting the soul: the testimony of the LORD is sure, making wise the simple. The statutes of the LORD are right, rejoicing the heart: the commandment of the LORD is pure, enlightening the eyes. The judgments of the LORD are true and righteous altogether.

Psalm 19:7-9 (KJV)

# GOD'S JUSTICE

He loves righteousness and justice; the earth is full of the goodness of the LORD.

Psalm 33:5 (NKJV)

Let those who delight in My righteousness shout for joy and be glad and say evermore, "Great is the LORD, who delights in the welfare of His servant!"

Psalm 35:27 (ESV)

For the LORD loveth judgment, and forsaketh not His saints; they are preserved for ever: but the seed of the wicked shall be cut off.

Psalm 37:28 (KJV)

He shall call to the heavens from above, and to the earth, that He may judge His people. Let the heavens declare His righteousness, for God Himself is Judge.

Psalm 50:4, 6 (NKJV)

# GOD'S JUSTICE

My mouth shall shew forth Thy righteousness and Thy salvation all the day; for I know not the numbers thereof. I will go in the strength of the Lord God: I will make mention of Thy righteousness, even of Thine only.

Psalm 71:15-16 (KJV)

Righteousness and justice are the foundation of Your throne; love and faithfulness go before You. They rejoice in Your name all day long; they exult in Your righteousness.

Psalm 89:14, 16 (NIV)

For He is coming, for He is coming to judge the earth. He shall judge the world with righteousness, and the peoples with His truth.

Psalm 96:13 (NKJV)

He will execute judgment among the nations, filling them with corpses; He will shatter chiefs over the wide earth.

Psalm 110:6 (ESV)

# GOD'S JUSTICE

All His commandments are sure. They stand fast for ever and ever, and are done in truth and uprightness.

Psalm 111:7-8 (KJV)

Righteous are You, O LORD, and upright are Your judgments. Your testimonies, which You have commanded, are righteous and very faithful.

Psalm 119:137-138 (NKJV)

The LORD is righteous; He has cut the cords of the wicked.

Psalm 129:4 (ESV)

For the LORD will judge His people, and He will repent himself concerning His servants.

Psalm 135:14 (NKJV)

The LORD is righteous in all His ways, and holy in all His works.

Psalm 145:17 (KJV)

# God's Majesty

For Thou hast maintained my right and my cause;
Thou satest in the throne judging right. But the
LORD shall endure for ever: He hath prepared His
throne for judgment. And He shall judge the world
in righteousness.

Psalm 9:4, 7-8 (KJV)

The LORD is King for ever and ever; the nations will
perish from His land.

Psalm 10:16 (NIV)

Lift up your heads, O gates! And be lifted up, O ancient doors, that the King of glory may come in. Who
is this King of glory? The LORD, strong and mighty, the
LORD, mighty in battle! Lift up your heads, O gates!
And lift them up, O ancient doors, that the King of
glory may come in. Who is this King of glory? The
LORD of hosts, He is the King of glory!

Psalm 24:7-10 (ESV)

# GOD'S MAJESTY

The LORD sits enthroned over the flood; the LORD is enthroned as King forever.

Psalm 29:10 (NIV)

For the LORD Most High is awesome; He is a great King over all the earth.

Psalm 47:2 (NKJV)

Sing praises to God, sing praises: sing praises unto our King, sing praises. For God is the King of all the earth: sing ye praises with understanding.

Psalm 47:6-7 (KJV)

Your procession is seen, O God, the procession of my God, my King, into the sanctuary – the singers in front, the musicians last, between them virgins playing tambourines: "Bless God in the great congregation, the LORD, O you who are of Israel's fountain!"

Psalm 68:24-26 (ESV)

# GOD'S MAJESTY

For God is my King of old, working salvation in the midst of the earth.

Psalm 74:12 (KJV)

For the LORD is the great God, the great King above all gods. In His hand are the depths of the earth, and the mountain peaks belong to Him. The sea is His, for He made it, and His hands formed the dry land. Come, let us bow down in worship, let us kneel before the LORD our Maker; for He is our God and we are the people of His pasture, the flock under His care.

Psalm 95:3-7 (NIV)

I will extol You, my God, O King; and I will bless Your name forever and ever.

Psalm 145:1 (NKJV)

Let Israel rejoice in Him that made him: let the children of Zion be joyful in their King.

Psalm 149:2 (KJV)

# GOD'S MERCY
## AND LOVE

Turn, O LORD, and deliver me; save me because of Your unfailing love.

Psalm 6:4 (NIV)

Remember, O LORD, Your tender mercies and Your lovingkindnesses, for they are from of old. Do not remember the sins of my youth, nor my transgressions; according to Your mercy remember me, for Your goodness' sake, O LORD.

Psalm 25:6-7 (NKJV)

Blessed be the LORD for He has heard the voice of my pleas for mercy.

Psalm 28:6 (ESV)

I have been young, and now am old; yet I have not seen the righteous forsaken, nor His descendants begging bread. He is ever merciful, and lends; and His descendants are blessed.

Psalm 37:25-26 (NKJV)

# GOD'S MERCY
# AND LOVE

Withhold not Thou Thy tender mercies from me, O LORD: let Thy lovingkindness and Thy truth continually preserve me.

Psalm 40:11 (KJV)

The LORD will command His lovingkindness in the daytime, and in the night His song shall be with me – a prayer to the God of my life.

Psalm 42:8 (NKJV)

Rise up and help us; redeem us because of Your unfailing love.

Psalm 44:26 (NIV)

Have mercy upon me, O God, according to Your lovingkindness; according to the multitude of Your tender mercies, blot out my transgressions.

Psalm 51:1 (NKJV)

# GOD'S MERCY AND LOVE

But I am like an olive tree flourishing in the house of God; I trust in God's unfailing love for ever and ever.

Psalm 52:8 (NIV)

Have mercy on me, O God, have mercy on me, for in You my soul takes refuge; I will take refuge in the shadow of Your wings until the disaster has passed.

Psalm 57:1 (NIV)

Because Your lovingkindness is better than life, my lips shall praise You.

Psalm 63:3 (NKJV)

Hear me, O LORD; for Thy lovingkindness is good: turn unto me according to the multitude of Thy tender mercies.

Psalm 69:16 (KJV)

# GOD'S MERCY
# AND LOVE

Has His steadfast love forever ceased? Are His promises at an end for all time?

Psalm 77:8 (ESV)

Be merciful unto me, O Lord: for I cry unto Thee daily. Rejoice the soul of Thy servant: for unto Thee, O Lord, do I lift up my soul. For Thou, Lord, art good, and ready to forgive; and plenteous in mercy unto all them that call upon Thee.

Psalm 86:3-5 (KJV)

For Your steadfast love is great above the heavens; Your faithfulness reaches to the clouds.

Psalm 108:4 (ESV)

The LORD is gracious and full of compassion, slow to anger and great in mercy. The LORD is good to all, and His tender mercies are over all His works.

Psalm 145:8-9 (NKJV)

# GOD'S PROTECTION

But Thou, O LORD, art a shield for me; my glory, and the lifter up of mine head.

Psalm 3:3 (KJV)

You have given me the shield of Your salvation, and Your right hand supported me, and Your gentleness made me great.

Psalm 18:35 (ESV)

Even though I walk through the valley of the shadow of death, I will fear no evil, for You are with me; Your rod and Your staff, they comfort me.

Psalm 23:4 (NIV)

Thou art my hiding place; Thou shalt preserve me from trouble; Thou shalt compass me about with songs of deliverance.

Psalm 32:7 (KJV)

# GOD'S PROTECTION

The LORD is my strength and my shield; in Him my heart trusts, and I am helped; my heart exults, and with my song I give thanks to Him.

Psalm 28:7 (ESV)

We wait in hope for the LORD; He is our help and our shield.

Psalm 33:20 (NIV)

I will cry unto God most high; unto God that performeth all things for me. He shall send from heaven, and save from the reproach of Him that would swallow me up. God shall send forth His mercy and His truth.

Psalm 57:2-3 (KJV)

Deliver me from my enemies, O my God; protect me from those who rise up against me.

Psalm 59:1 (ESV)

# GOD'S PROTECTION

Behold, O God our shield, and look upon the face of Thine anointed. For the LORD God is a sun and shield: the LORD will give grace and glory: no good thing will He withhold from them that walk uprightly.

Psalm 84:9, 11 (KJV)

He will cover you with His pinions, and under His wings you will find refuge; His faithfulness is a shield and buckler.

Psalm 91:4 (ESV)

"Because he loves me," says the LORD, "I will rescue him; I will protect him, for he acknowledges My name. He will call upon Me, and I will answer him; I will be with him in trouble, I will deliver him and honor him."

Psalm 91:14-15 (NIV)

# GOD'S PROTECTION

You who fear the LORD, trust in the LORD! He is their help and their shield.

Psalm 115:11 (ESV)

Thou art my hiding place and my shield: I hope in Thy word.

Psalm 119:114 (KJV)

The LORD watches over you – the LORD is your shade at your right hand; the sun will not harm you by day, nor the moon by night. The LORD will keep you from all harm – He will watch over your life; the LORD will watch over your coming and going both now and forevermore.

Psalm 121:5-8 (NIV)

As the mountains surround Jerusalem, so the LORD surrounds His people from this time forth and forever.

Psalm 125:2 (NKJV)

# GOD'S PROTECTION

Unless the LORD builds the house, its builders labor in vain. Unless the LORD watches over the city, the watchmen stand guard in vain.

Psalm 127:1 (NIV)

Though I walk in the midst of trouble, You preserve my life; You stretch out Your hand against the wrath of my enemies, and Your right hand delivers me.

Psalm 138:7 (ESV)

Keep me, O LORD, from the hands of the wicked; preserve me from the violent man; who have purposed to overthrow my goings.

Psalm 140:4 (KJV)

Blessed be the LORD my Rock, who trains my hands for war, and my fingers for battle – my lovingkindness and my fortress, my high tower and my deliverer, my shield and the One in whom I take refuge.

Psalm 144:1-2 (NKJV)

# God's Word

The words of the LORD are pure words, like silver tried in a furnace of earth, purified seven times.

Psalm 12:6 (NKJV)

As for the deeds of men – by the word of Your lips I have kept myself from the ways of the violent.

Psalm 17:4 (NIV)

This God – His way is perfect; the word of the LORD proves true; He is a shield for all those who take refuge in Him.

Psalm 18:30 (ESV)

The statutes of the LORD are right, rejoicing the heart; the commandment of the LORD is pure, enlightening the eyes.

Psalm 19:8 (NKJV)

# GOD'S WORD

For the word of the LORD is right; and all His works are done in truth.

Psalm 33:4 (KJV)


For with You is the fountain of life; in Your light we see light.

Psalm 36:9 (NKJV)


Send out Your light and Your truth; let them lead me; let them bring me to Your holy hill and to Your dwelling!

Psalm 43:3 (ESV)


The Lord announced the word, and great was the company of those who proclaimed it.

Psalm 68:11 (NIV)


I will not violate my covenant or alter the word that went forth from my lips.

Psalm 89:34 (ESV)

# GOD'S WORD

He remembers His covenant forever, the word which He commanded, for a thousand generations.

Psalm 105:8 (NKJV)

He sent His word, and healed them, and delivered them from their destructions.

Psalm 107:20 (KJV)

How can a young man keep his way pure? By living according to Your word. I seek You with all my heart; do not let me stray from Your commands. I have hidden Your word in my heart that I might not sin against You.

Psalm 119:9-11 (NIV)

Your word is a lamp to my feet and a light to my path.

Psalm 119:105 (ESV)

# GOSSIP

Thou shalt destroy them that speak leasing: the LORD will abhor the bloody and deceitful man.

Psalm 5:6 (KJV)

Save, O LORD, for the godly one is gone; for the faithful have vanished from among the children of man. Everyone utters lies to his neighbor; with flattering lips and a double heart they speak. May the LORD cut off all flattering lips, the tongue that makes great boasts, those who say, "With our tongue we will prevail, our lips are with us; who is master over us?"

Psalm 12:1-4 (ESV)

May the words of my mouth and the meditation of my heart be pleasing in Your sight, O LORD, my Rock and my Redeemer.

Psalm 19:14 (NIV)

# GOSSIP

Let the lying lips be put to silence, which speak insolent things proudly and contemptuously against the righteous.

Psalm 31:18 (NKJV)

Keep thy tongue from evil, and thy lips from speaking guile.

Psalm 34:13 (KJV)

The mouth of the righteous speaks wisdom, and his tongue talks of justice.

Psalm 37:30 (NKJV)

Let my mouth be filled with Thy praise and with Thy honour all the day.

Psalm 71:8 (KJV)

Set a guard, O LORD, over my mouth; keep watch over the door of my lips!

Psalm 141:3 (ESV)

# GOVERNMENT

Now therefore, be wise, O kings; be instructed, you judges of the earth. Serve the LORD with fear, and rejoice with trembling. Kiss the Son, lest He be angry, and you perish in the way, when His wrath is kindled but a little. Blessed are all those who put their trust in Him.

Psalm 2:10-12 (NKJV)

For the king trusts in the LORD; through the unfailing love of the Most High he will not be shaken.

Psalm 21:7 (NIV)

For I will not trust in my bow, neither shall my sword save me. But Thou hast saved us from our enemies, and hast put them to shame that hated us. In God we boast all the day long, and praise Thy name for ever.

Psalm 44:6-8 (KJV)

# Government

Can wicked rulers be allied with You, those who frame injustice by statute? They band together against the life of the righteous and condemn the innocent to death. But the LORD has become my stronghold, and my God the rock of my refuge. He will bring back on them their iniquity and wipe them out for their wickedness.

Psalm 94:20-23 (ESV)

For all the gods of the peoples are idols, but the LORD made the heavens.

Psalm 96:5 (NKJV)

It is better to trust in the LORD than to put confidence in man. It is better to trust in the LORD than to put confidence in princes.

Psalm 118:8-9 (KJV)

The LORD will reign forever, your God, O Zion, to all generations. Praise the LORD!

Psalm 146:10 (ESV)

# Help and Comfort

O Lord, You hear the desire of the afflicted; You will strengthen their heart; You will incline Your ear to do justice to the fatherless and the oppressed, so that man who is of the earth may strike terror no more.

Psalm 10:17-18 (esv)

Yea, though I walk through the valley of the shadow of death, I will fear no evil; for You are with me; Your rod and Your staff, they comfort me.

Psalm 23:4 (nkjv)

How great is Your goodness, which You have stored up for those who fear You, which You bestow in the sight of men on those who take refuge in You. Be strong and take heart, all you who hope in the Lord.

Psalm 31:19, 24 (niv)

# HELP AND COMFORT

And the LORD shall help them and deliver them: he shall deliver them from the wicked, and save them, because they trust in Him.

Psalm 37:40 (KJV)

Yet I am poor and needy; may the Lord think of me. You are my help and my deliverer; O my God, do not delay.

Psalm 40:17 (NIV)

God is our refuge and strength, a very present help in trouble. Therefore we will not fear, even though the earth be removed, and though the mountains be carried into the midst of the sea; the LORD of hosts is with us; the God of Jacob is our refuge.

Psalm 46:1-2, 7 (NKJV)

Make haste, O God, to deliver me; make haste to help me, O LORD.

Psalm 70:1 (KJV)

# HELP AND COMFORT

Thou shalt increase my greatness, and comfort me on every side.

Psalm 71:21 (KJV)


Help us, O God of our salvation, for the glory of Your name; and deliver us, and provide atonement for our sins, for Your name's sake.

Psalm 79:9 (NKJV)


If the LORD had not been my help, my soul would soon have lived in the land of silence.

Psalm 94:17 (ESV)


Give us help from trouble, for the help of man is useless.

Psalm 108:12 (NKJV)


Help me, O LORD my God; save me in accordance with Your love.

Psalm 109:26 (NIV)

# HELP AND COMFORT

O house of Israel, trust in the LORD – He is their help and shield. O house of Aaron, trust in the LORD – He is their help and shield. You who fear Him, trust in the LORD – He is their help and shield.

Psalm 115:9-11 (NIV)

The LORD is on my side; I will not fear: what can man do unto me?

Psalm 118:6 (KJV)

My comfort in my suffering is this: Your promise preserves my life. May Your unfailing love be my comfort, according to Your promise to Your servant.

Psalm 119:50, 76 (NIV)

The LORD is near to all who call on Him, to all who call on Him in truth. He fulfills the desire of those who fear Him; He also hears their cry and saves them.

Psalm 145:18-19 (ESV)

# Joy

But let all who take refuge in You rejoice; let them ever sing for joy, and spread Your protection over them, that those who love Your name may exult in You.

Psalm 5:11 (ESV)


Thou wilt shew me the path of life: in Thy presence is fulness of joy; at Thy right hand there are pleasures for evermore.

Psalm 16:11 (KJV)


Then my head will be exalted above the enemies who surround me; at His tabernacle will I sacrifice with shouts of joy; I will sing and make music to the LORD.

Psalm 27:6 (NIV)


For His anger lasts only a moment, but His favor lasts a lifetime; weeping may remain for a night, but rejoicing comes in the morning.

Psalm 30:5 (NIV)

# JOY

Be glad in the LORD, and rejoice, O righteous, and shout for joy, all you upright in heart!

Psalm 32:11 (ESV)

Let them shout for joy and be glad, who favor my righteous cause; and let them say continually, "Let the LORD be magnified, who has pleasure in the prosperity of His servant."

Psalm 35:27 (NKJV)

But may all who seek You rejoice and be glad in You; may those who love Your salvation say continually, "Great is the LORD!"

Psalm 40:16 (ESV)

Clap your hands, all you nations; shout to God with cries of joy. How awesome is the LORD Most High, the great King over all the earth!

Psalm 47:1-2 (NIV)

# Joy

Let mount Zion rejoice, let the daughters of Judah be glad, because of thy judgments.

Psalm 48:11 (KJV)

My soul shall be satisfied as with marrow and fatness; and my mouth shall praise Thee with joyful lips: When I remember Thee upon my bed, and meditate on Thee in the night watches. Because Thou hast been my help, therefore in the shadow of Thy wings will I rejoice.

Psalm 63:5-7 (KJV)

Let the righteous rejoice in the LORD and take refuge in Him; let all the upright in heart praise Him!

Psalm 64:10 (NIV)

Oh, let the nations be glad and sing for joy! For You shall judge the people righteously, and govern the nations on earth.

Psalm 67:3-4 (NKJV)

# JOY

The righteous shall be glad; they shall exult before God; they shall be jubilant with joy!

Psalm 68:3 (ESV)

Let all those who seek You rejoice and be glad in You; and let those who love Your salvation say continually, "Let God be magnified!"

Psalm 70:4 (NKJV)

Serve the LORD with gladness: come before His presence with singing.

Psalm 100:2 (KJV)

This is the day the LORD has made; let us rejoice and be glad in it.

Psalm 118:24 (NIV)

Let the saints be joyful in glory; let them sing aloud on their beds.

Psalm 149:5 (NKJV)

# LONG LIFE

You have made known to me the path of life; You will fill me with joy in Your presence, with eternal pleasures at Your right hand.

Psalm 16:11 (NIV)

He asked life from You, and You gave it to him – length of days forever and ever.

Psalm 21:4 (NKJV)

One thing I ask of the LORD, this is what I seek: that I may dwell in the house of the LORD all the days of my life, to gaze upon the beauty of the LORD and to seek Him in His temple.

Psalm 27:4 (NIV)

My times are in Thy hand: deliver me from the hand of mine enemies, and from them that persecute me.

Psalm 31:15 (KJV)

# Long life

O Lord, make me know my end and what is the measure of my days; let me know how fleeting I am! Behold, You have made my days a few handbreadths, and my lifetime is as nothing before You. Surely all mankind stands as a mere breath!

Psalm 39:4-5 (esv)

Do not cast me off in the time of old age; do not forsake me when my strength fails.

Psalm 71:9 (nkjv)

Since my youth, O God, You have taught me, and to this day I declare Your marvelous deeds. Even when I am old and gray, do not forsake me, O God, till I declare Your power to the next generation, Your might to all who are to come.

Psalm 71:17-18 (niv)

# LOVING GOD

But let all those that put their trust in Thee rejoice: let them ever shout for joy, because Thou defendest them: let them also that love Thy name be joyful in Thee.

Psalm 5:11 (KJV)

I love You, O LORD, my strength. The LORD is my rock and my fortress and my deliverer, my God, my rock, in whom I take refuge.

Psalm 18:1-2 (ESV)

Oh, love the LORD, all you His saints! For the LORD preserves the faithful, and fully repays the proud person.

Psalm 31:23 (NKJV)

But may all who seek You rejoice and be glad in You; may those who love Your salvation always say, "The LORD be exalted!"

Psalm 40:16 (NIV)

# Loving God

For God will save Zion, and will build the cities of Judah: that they may dwell there, and have it in possession. The seed also of His servants shall inherit it: and they that love His name shall dwell therein.

Psalm 69:35-36 (KJV)

Let all those who seek You rejoice and be glad in You; and let those who love Your salvation say continually, "Let God be magnified!"

Psalm 70:4 (NKJV)

Because he holds fast to Me in love, I will deliver him; I will protect him, because he knows My name.

Psalm 91:14 (ESV)

Ye that love the LORD, hate evil: He preserveth the souls of His saints; He delivereth them out of the hand of the wicked.

Psalm 97:10 (KJV)

# LOVING GOD

I love the LORD, because He hath heard my voice and my supplications.

Psalm 116:1 (KJV)

Therefore I love Your commandments above gold, above fine gold.

Psalm 119:127 (ESV)

Look upon me and be merciful to me, as Your custom is toward those who love Your name.

Psalm 119:132 (NKJV)

Great peace have they which love Thy law: and nothing shall offend them.

Psalm 119:165 (KJV)

The LORD watches over all who love Him, but all the wicked He will destroy.

Psalm 145:20 (NIV)

# PATIENCE

Wait on the LORD; be of good courage, and He shall strengthen your heart; wait, I say, on the LORD!

Psalm 27:14 (NKJV)

Our soul waits for the LORD; He is our help and our shield. For our heart is glad in Him, because we trust in His holy name.

Psalm 33:20-21 (ESV)

Wait for the LORD and keep His way. He will exalt you to inherit the land; when the wicked are cut off, you will see it.

Psalm 37:34 (NIV)

I waited patiently for the LORD; He inclined to me and heard my cry.

Psalm 40:1 (ESV)

# PATIENCE

My soul, wait thou only upon God; for my expectation is from Him.

Psalm 62:5 (KJV)

These all wait for You, that You may give them their food in due season.

Psalm 104:27 (NKJV)

Behold, as the eyes of servants look to the hand of their master, as the eyes of a maidservant to the hand of her mistress, so our eyes look to the LORD our God, till He has mercy upon us.

Psalm 123:2 (ESV)

I wait for the LORD, my soul doth wait, and in His word do I hope. My soul waiteth for the Lord more than they that watch for the morning: I say, more than they that watch for the morning.

Psalm 130:5-6 (KJV)

# PEACE

I will both lie down in peace, and sleep; for You alone, O LORD, make me dwell in safety.

Psalm 4:8 (NKJV)

He makes me lie down in green pastures, He leads me beside quiet waters, He restores my soul.

Psalm 23:2-3 (NIV)

The LORD will give strength unto His people; the LORD will bless His people with peace.

Psalm 29:11 (KJV)

Turn from evil and do good; seek peace and pursue it.

Psalm 34:14 (NIV)

Be still before the LORD and wait patiently for Him; fret not yourself over the one who prospers in his way, over the man who carries out evil devices!

Psalm 37:7 (ESV)

# PEACE

But the meek shall inherit the earth, and shall delight themselves in the abundance of peace.

Psalm 37:11 (NKJV)

Mark the blameless and behold the upright, for there is a future for the man of peace.

Psalm 37:37 (ESV)

"Be still, and know that I am God; I will be exalted among the nations, I will be exalted in the earth."

Psalm 46:10 (NIV)

In His days shall the righteous flourish; and abundance of peace so long as the moon endureth.

Psalm 72:7 (KJV)

Great peace have those who love Your law, and nothing causes them to stumble.

Psalm 119:165 (NKJV)

# PRAISE AND WORSHIP

The LORD lives, and blessed be my rock, and exalted be the God of my salvation – for this I will praise You, O LORD, among the nations, and sing to Your name.

Psalm 18:46, 49 (ESV)

Be exalted, O LORD, in Your own strength! We will sing and praise Your power.

Psalm 21:13 (NKJV)

My praise shall be of Thee in the great congregation: I will pay my vows before them that fear Him.

Psalm 22:25 (KJV)

Ascribe to the LORD, O mighty ones, ascribe to the LORD glory and strength. Ascribe to the LORD the glory due His name; worship the LORD in the splendor of His holiness.

Psalm 29:1-2 (NIV)

# PRAISE AND WORSHIP

Sing to the LORD, you saints of His; praise His holy name.

Psalm 30:4 (NIV)

Sing joyfully to the LORD, you righteous; it is fitting for the upright to praise Him. Praise the LORD with the harp; make music to Him on the ten-stringed lyre. Sing to Him a new song; play skillfully, and shout for joy.

Psalm 33:1-3 (NIV)

I will give you thanks in the great assembly; among throngs of people I will praise You.

Psalm 35:18 (NIV)

I will make Thy name to be remembered in all generations: therefore shall the people praise Thee for ever and ever.

Psalm 45:17 (KJV)

# PRAISE AND WORSHIP

Oh, clap your hands, all you peoples! Shout to God with the voice of triumph! For the LORD Most High is awesome; He is a great King over all the earth. Sing praises to God, sing praises! Sing praises to our King, sing praises! For God is the King of all the earth.

Psalm 47:1-2, 6-7 (NKJV)

Because Your steadfast love is better than life, my lips will praise You. So I will bless You as long as I live; in Your name I will lift up my hands.

Psalm 63:3-4 (ESV)

I cried unto Him with my mouth, and He was extolled with my tongue.

Psalm 66:17 (KJV)

We give thanks to You, O God, we give thanks, for Your Name is near; men tell of Your wonderful deeds.

Psalm 75:1 (NIV)

86

# PRAISE AND WORSHIP

Among the gods there is none like You, O Lord; no deeds can compare with Yours. For You are great and do marvelous deeds; You alone are God.

Psalm 86:8, 10 (NIV)

Enter His gates with thanksgiving and His courts with praise; give thanks to Him and praise His name.

Psalm 100:4 (NIV)

Praise the Lord! Praise, O servants of the Lord, praise the name of the Lord! Blessed be the name of the Lord from this time forth and forevermore!

Psalm 113:1-2 (ESV)

I will extol You, my God, O King; and I will bless Your name forever and ever. Every day I will bless You, and I will praise Your name forever and ever.

Psalm 145:1-2 (NKJV)

# PRAYER

Hear me when I call, O God of my righteousness: Thou hast enlarged me when I was in distress; have mercy upon me, and hear my prayer.

Psalm 4:1 (KJV)

The LORD has heard my supplication; the LORD will receive my prayer.

Psalm 6:9 (NKJV)

Hear, O LORD, my righteous plea; listen to my cry. Give ear to my prayer – it does not rise from deceitful lips.

Psalm 17:1 (NIV)

Therefore let everyone who is godly offer prayer to You at a time when You may be found. You are a hiding place for me; you preserve me from trouble; you surround me with shouts of deliverance.

Psalm 32:6-7 (ESV)

# PRAYER

Hear my prayer, O LORD, and give ear to my cry; hold not Your peace at my tears! For I am a sojourner with You, a guest, like all my fathers.

Psalm 39:12 (ESV)

The LORD will command His lovingkindness in the daytime, and in the night His song shall be with me – a prayer to the God of my life.

Psalm 42:8 (NKJV)

Hear my prayer, O God; listen to the words of my mouth.

Psalm 54:2 (NIV)

Give ear to my prayer, O God, and hide not Yourself from my plea for mercy!

Psalm 55:1 (ESV)

Hear my cry, O God; attend unto my prayer.

Psalm 61:1 (KJV)

# PRAYER

O You who hear prayer, to You all men will come.

Psalm 65:2 (NIV)

But truly God has listened; He has attended to the voice of my prayer. Blessed be God, because He has not rejected my prayer or removed His steadfast love from me!

Psalm 66:19-20 (ESV)

But as for me, my prayer is unto Thee, O LORD, in an acceptable time: O God, in the multitude of Thy mercy hear me, in the truth of Thy salvation.

Psalm 69:13 (KJV)

My soul longs, yes, even faints for the courts of the LORD; my heart and my flesh cry out for the living God. O LORD God of hosts, hear my prayer; give ear, O God of Jacob.

Psalm 84:2, 8 (NKJV)

# PRAYER

O Lord, God of my salvation, I have cried out day and night before You. Let my prayer come before You; incline Your ear to my cry.

Psalm 88:1-2 (NKJV)

Hear my prayer, O Lord; let my cry come to You! Do not hide Your face from me in the day of my distress! Incline Your ear to me; answer me speedily in the day when I call! For the Lord builds up Zion; He appears in His glory; He regards the prayer of the destitute and does not despise their prayer.

Psalm 102:1-2, 16-17 (ESV)

May my prayer be set before You like incense; may the lifting up of my hands be like the evening sacrifice.

Psalm 141:2 (NIV)

# PRIDE

The boastful shall not stand before Your eyes; You hate all evildoers.

Psalm 5:5 (ESV)

When He maketh inquisition for blood, He remembereth them: He forgetteth not the cry of the humble.

Psalm 9:12 (KJV)

For the wicked boasts of his heart's desire; He blesses the greedy and renounces the LORD. The wicked in his proud countenance does not seek God. LORD, You have heard the desire of the humble; You will prepare their heart; You will cause Your ear to hear.

Psalm 10:3-4, 17 (NKJV)

The meek shall eat and be satisfied: they shall praise the LORD that seek Him: your heart shall live for ever.

Psalm 22:26 (KJV)

# PRIDE

But the meek shall inherit the land and delight themselves in abundant peace.

Psalm 37:11 (ESV)

Blessed is the man who makes the LORD his trust, who does not look to the proud.

Psalm 40:4 (NIV)

For Thou desirest not sacrifice; else would I give it: Thou delightest not in burnt offering. The sacrifices of God are a broken spirit: a broken and a contrite heart, O God, Thou wilt not despise.

Psalm 51:16-17 (KJV)

Though the LORD is on high, He looks upon the lowly, but the proud He knows from afar.

Psalm 138:6 (NIV)

For the LORD takes pleasure in His people; He adorns the humble with salvation.

Psalm 149:4 (ESV)

# REDEMPTION

With the pure You will show Yourself pure; and with the devious You will show Yourself shrewd. For You will save the humble people, but will bring down haughty looks.

Psalm 18:26-27 (NKJV)

But as for me, I shall walk in my integrity; redeem me, and be gracious to me.

Psalm 26:11 (ESV)

Make Thy face to shine upon Thy servant: save me for Thy mercies' sake.

Psalm 31:16 (KJV)

No man can redeem the life of another or give to God a ransom for him – the ransom for a life is costly, no payment is ever enough – that he should live on forever and not see decay.

Psalm 49:7-9 (NIV)

94

# REDEMPTION

And do not hide Your face from Your servant, for I am in trouble; hear me speedily. Draw near to my soul, and redeem it; deliver me because of my enemies.

Psalm 69:17-18 (NKJV)

Rescue me and deliver me in Your righteousness; turn Your ear to me and save me. Be my rock of refuge, to which I can always go; give the command to save me, for You are my rock and my fortress.

Psalm 71:2-3 (NIV)

From oppression and violence He redeems their life, and precious is their blood in His sight.

Psalm 72:14 (ESV)

Preserve my soul; for I am holy: O Thou my God, save Thy servant that trusteth in Thee.

Psalm 86:2 (KJV)

# REDEMPTION

Save us, O LORD our God, and gather us from among the nations, that we may give thanks to Your holy name and glory in Your praise.

Psalm 106:47 (ESV)

With my mouth I will greatly extol the LORD; in the great throng I will praise Him. For He stands at the right hand of the needy one, to save his life from those who condemn him.

Psalm 109:30-31 (NIV)

He sent redemption unto His people: He hath commanded His covenant for ever: holy and reverend is His name.

Psalm 111:9 (KJV)

O Israel, hope in the LORD; for with the LORD there is mercy, and with Him is abundant redemption.

Psalm 130:7 (NKJV)

# REPENTANCE

Answer me when I call, O God of my righteousness! You have given me relief when I was in distress. Be gracious to me and hear my prayer!

Psalm 4:1 (ESV)

Turn, O Lord, and deliver me; save me because of Your unfailing love. The Lord has heard my cry for mercy; the Lord accepts my prayer.

Psalm 6:4, 9 (NIV)

If a man does not repent, God will whet His sword; He has bent and readied His bow.

Psalm 7:12 (ESV)

For Thy name's sake, O Lord, pardon mine iniquity; for it is great. Look upon mine affliction and my pain; and forgive all my sins.

Psalm 25:11, 18 (KJV)

# REPENTANCE

I acknowledged my sin to You, and I did not cover my iniquity; I said, "I will confess my transgressions to the LORD," and You forgave the iniquity of my sin.

Psalm 32:5 (ESV)

Wash me thoroughly from my iniquity, and cleanse me from my sin. For I acknowledge my transgressions, and my sin is always before me.

Psalm 51:2-3 (NKJV)

Restore unto me the joy of Thy salvation; and uphold me with Thy free spirit. Then will I teach transgressors Thy ways; and sinners shall be converted unto Thee. Deliver me from bloodguiltiness, O God, Thou God of my salvation: and my tongue shall sing aloud of Thy righteousness.

Psalm 51:12-14 (KJV)

# Repentance

Iniquities prevail against me: as for our transgressions, Thou shalt purge them away.

Psalm 65:3 (KJV)

Help us, O God of our salvation, for the glory of Your name; deliver us, and atone for our sins, for Your name's sake!

Psalm 79:9 (ESV)

For as the heavens are high above the earth, so great is His mercy toward those who fear Him; as far as the east is from the west, so far has He removed our transgressions from us.

Psalm 103:11-12 (NKJV)

Search me, O God, and know my heart: try me, and know my thoughts: And see if there be any wicked way in me, and lead me in the way everlasting.

Psalm 139:23-24 (KJV)

# REVERENCE

Serve the LORD with fear, and rejoice with trembling.
Psalm 2:11 (KJV)

I, through the abundance of Your steadfast love, will enter Your house. I will bow down toward Your holy temple in the fear of You.

Psalm 5:7 (ESV)

The fear of the LORD is clean, enduring for ever: the judgments of the LORD are true and righteous altogether.

Psalm 19:9 (KJV)

But You are holy, enthroned in the praises of Israel.
Psalm 22:3 (NKJV)

You who fear the LORD, praise Him! All you descendants of Jacob, honor Him! Revere Him, all you descendants of Israel!

Psalm 22:23 (NIV)

# REVERENCE

How great is Your goodness, which You have stored up for those who fear You, which You bestow in the sight of men on those who take refuge in You.

Psalm 31:19 (NIV)

Let all the earth fear the LORD; let all the inhabitants of the world stand in awe of Him. For He spoke, and it was done; He commanded, and it stood fast.

Psalm 33:8-9 (NKJV)

In Your majesty ride out victoriously for the cause of truth and meekness and righteousness; let Your right hand teach You awesome deeds!

Psalm 45:4 (ESV)

God shall bless us; and all the ends of the earth shall fear Him.

Psalm 67:7 (KJV)

# REVERENCE

O God, You are more awesome than Your holy places. The God of Israel is He who gives strength and power to His people.

Psalm 68:35 (NKJV)

For who in the heavens can be compared to the LORD? Who among the sons of the mighty can be likened to the LORD? God is greatly to be feared in the assembly of the saints, and to be held in reverence by all those around Him.

Psalm 89:6-7 (NKJV)

Worship the LORD in the splendor of holiness; tremble before Him, all the earth!

Psalm 96:9 (ESV)

Let them praise Thy great and terrible name; for it is holy. Exalt ye the LORD our God, and worship at His footstool; for He is holy.

Psalm 99:3, 5 (KJV)

# REVERENCE

For as high as the heavens are above the earth, so great is His steadfast love toward those who fear Him. As a father shows compassion to his children, so the LORD shows compassion to those who fear Him. But the steadfast love of the LORD is from everlasting to everlasting on those who fear Him, and His righteousness to children's children.

Psalm 103:11, 13, 17 (ESV)

He provides food for those who fear Him; He remembers His covenant forever. He sent redemption to His people; He has commanded His covenant forever. Holy and awesome is His name!

Psalm 111:5, 9 (ESV)

My mouth will speak in praise of the LORD. Let every creature praise His holy name for ever and ever.

Psalm 145:21 (NIV)

# RIGHTEOUSNESS

For You bless the righteous, O LORD; You cover him with favor as with a shield.

Psalm 5:12 (ESV)

The LORD tests the righteous, but the wicked and the one who loves violence His soul hates.

Psalm 11:5 (NKJV)

The eyes of the LORD are on the righteous, and His ears are open to their cry. The face of the LORD is against those who do evil, to cut off the remembrance of them from the earth. The righteous cry out, and the LORD hears, and delivers them out of all their troubles.

Psalm 34:15-17 (NKJV)

Many are the afflictions of the righteous: but the LORD delivereth him out of them all. Evil shall slay the wicked: and they that hate the righteous shall be desolate.

Psalm 34:19, 21 (KJV)

# RIGHTEOUSNESS

Better the little that the righteous have than the wealth of many wicked; for the power of the wicked will be broken, but the LORD upholds the righteous.

Psalm 37:16-17 (NIV)

The salvation of the righteous is from the LORD; He is their strength in the time of trouble.

Psalm 37:39 (NKJV)

Cast your burden on the LORD, and He will sustain you; He will never permit the righteous to be moved.

Psalm 55:22 (ESV)

In His days the righteous will flourish; prosperity will abound till the moon is no more.

Psalm 72:7 (NIV)

The righteous shall flourish like the palm tree: he shall grow like a cedar in Lebanon.

Psalm 92:12 (KJV)

# RIGHTEOUSNESS

Light is sown for the righteous, and gladness for the upright in heart. Rejoice in the LORD, you righteous, and give thanks at the remembrance of His holy name.

Psalm 97:11-12 (NKJV)

Blessed is the man who fears the LORD, who finds great delight in His commands. Even in darkness light dawns for the upright, for the gracious and compassionate and righteous man.

Psalm 112:1, 4 (NIV)

Let a righteous man strike me – it is a kindness; let him rebuke me – it is oil for my head; let my head not refuse it.

Psalm 141:5 (ESV)

# SIN

In your anger do not sin; when you are on your beds, search your hearts and be silent.

Psalm 4:4 (NIV)

For the wicked boasts of the desires of his soul, and the one greedy for gain curses and renounces the LORD.

Psalm 10:3 (ESV)

Keep back Thy servant also from presumptuous sins; let them not have dominion over me: then shall I be upright, and I shall be innocent from the great transgression.

Psalm 19:13 (KJV)

Do not remember the sins of my youth, nor my transgressions; according to Your mercy remember me, for Your goodness' sake, O LORD.

Psalm 25:7 (NKJV)

# SIN

A little while, and the wicked will be no more; though you look for them, they will not be found.

Psalm 37:10 (NIV)

There is no soundness in my flesh because of Your indignation; there is no health in my bones because of my sin.

Psalm 38:3 (ESV)

I said, I will take heed to my ways, that I sin not with my tongue: I will keep my mouth with a bridle, while the wicked is before me.

Psalm 39:1 (KJV)

Deliver me from all my transgressions; do not make me the reproach of the foolish.

Psalm 39:8 (NKJV)

Wash me thoroughly from my iniquity, and cleanse me from my sin!

Psalm 51:2 (ESV)

# SIN

Behold, I was shapen in iniquity; and in sin did my mother conceive me.

Psalm 51:5 (KJV)

As smoke is driven away, so drive them away: as wax melteth before the fire, so let the wicked perish at the presence of God.

Psalm 68:2 (KJV)

For indeed, those who are far from You shall perish; You have destroyed all those who desert You for harlotry. But it is good for me to draw near to God; I have put my trust in the Lord GOD, that I may declare all Your works.

Psalm 73:27-28 (NKJV)

You forgave the iniquity of Your people; You covered all their sin.

Psalm 85:2 (ESV)

# SIN

He will not always accuse, nor will He harbor His anger forever; He does not treat us as our sins deserve or repay us according to our iniquities. For as high as the heavens are above the earth, so great is His love for those who fear Him; as far as the east is from the west, so far has He removed our transgressions from us.

Psalm 103:9-12 (NIV)

With my whole heart I have sought You; oh, let me not wander from Your commandments! Your word I have hidden in my heart, that I might not sin against You.

Psalm 119:10-11 (NKJV)

The LORD preserveth the strangers; He relieveth the fatherless and widow: but the way of the wicked He turneth upside down.

Psalm 146:9 (KJV)

# THE NEEDY

But the needy will not always be forgotten, nor the hope of the afflicted ever perish.

Psalm 9:18 (NIV)

"For the oppression of the poor, for the sighing of the needy, now I will arise," says the LORD; "I will set him in the safety for which he yearns."

Psalm 12:5 (NKJV)

This poor man cried, and the LORD heard him and saved him out of all his troubles.

Psalm 34:6 (ESV)

Blessed is he that considereth the poor: the LORD will deliver him in time of trouble.

Psalm 41:1 (KJV)

But I am poor and needy; yet the LORD thinks upon me. You are my help and my deliverer; do not delay, O my God.

Psalm 40:17 (NKJV)

# THE NEEDY

O LORD, who is like You, delivering the poor from him who is too strong for him, the poor and needy from him who robs him?

Psalm 35:10 (ESV)

For He will deliver the needy who cry out, the afflicted who have no one to help. He will take pity on the weak and the needy and save the needy from death. He will rescue them from oppression and violence, for precious is their blood in His sight.

Psalm 72:12-14 (NIV)

Defend the poor and fatherless; do justice to the afflicted and needy. Deliver the poor and needy; free them from the hand of the wicked.

Psalm 82:3-4 (NKJV)

He raiseth up the poor out of the dust, and lifteth the needy out of the dunghill.

Psalm 113:7 (KJV)

# TRUST

Offer the sacrifices of righteousness, and put your trust in the LORD.

Psalm 4:5 (KJV)

Those who know Your name will trust in You, for You, LORD, have never forsaken those who seek You.

Psalm 9:10 (NIV)

I have set the LORD always before me; because He is at my right hand, I shall not be shaken.

Psalm 16:8 (ESV)

Some trust in chariots, and some in horses; but we will remember the name of the LORD our God.

Psalm 20:7 (NKJV)

You brought me out of the womb; You made me trust in You even at my mother's breast.

Psalm 22:9 (NIV)

# TRUST

O my God, in You I trust; let me not be put to shame; let not my enemies exult over me.

Psalm 25:2 (ESV)

I have hated them that regard lying vanities: but I trust in the LORD.

Psalm 31:6 (KJV)

But I trust in You, O LORD; I say, "You are my God."

Psalm 31:14 (NIV)

Many sorrows shall be to the wicked: but he that trusteth in the LORD, mercy shall compass him about.

Psalm 32:10 (KJV)

Trust in the LORD, and do good; dwell in the land, and feed on His faithfulness. Delight yourself also in the LORD, and He shall give you the desires of your heart.

Psalm 37:3-4 (NKJV)

# TRUST

When I am afraid, I will trust in You. In God, whose word I praise, in God I trust; I will not be afraid. What can mortal man do to me?

Psalm 56:3-4 (NIV)

Trust in Him at all times; pour out your heart before Him: God is a refuge for us.

Psalm 62:8 (KJV)

For Thou art my hope, O Lord God: Thou art my trust from my youth.

Psalm 71:5 (KJV)

O Lord Almighty, blessed is the man who trusts in You.

Psalm 84:12 (NIV)

Let Your steadfast love come to me, O Lord, Your salvation according to Your promise; then shall I have an answer for him who taunts me, for I trust in Your word.

Psalm 119:41-42 (ESV)

# TRUST

Teach me good judgment and knowledge, for I believe Your commandments.

Psalm 119:66 (NKJV)

Those who trust in the LORD are like Mount Zion, which cannot be moved, but abides forever.

Psalm 125:1 (NKJV)

Let me hear in the morning of Your steadfast love, for in You I trust. Make me know the way I should go, for to You I lift up my soul.

Psalm 143:8 (ESV)

Do not put your trust in princes, in mortal men, who cannot save. Blessed is he whose help is the God of Jacob, whose hope is in the LORD his God.

Psalm 146:3, 5 (NIV)

# TRUST

Not a word from their mouth can be trusted; their heart is filled with destruction. Their throat is an open grave; with their tongue they speak deceit. Declare them guilty, O God!

Psalm 5:9-10 (NIV)

LORD, who may abide in Your tabernacle? Who may dwell in Your holy hill? He who walks uprightly, and works righteousness, and speaks the truth in his heart.

Psalm 15:1-2 (NKJV)

Lead me in Your truth and teach me, for You are the God of my salvation; for You I wait all the day long.

Psalm 25:5 (ESV)

O send out Thy light and Thy truth: let them lead me; let them bring me unto Thy holy hill, and to Thy tabernacles.

Psalm 43:3 (KJV)

# Truth

Behold, Thou desirest truth in the inward parts: and in the hidden part Thou shalt make me to know wisdom.

Psalm 51:6 (KJV)


The wicked are estranged from the womb; they go astray from birth, speaking lies.

Psalm 58:3 (ESV)


For the sins of their mouths, for the words of their lips, let them be caught in their pride. For the curses and lies they utter, consume them in wrath, consume them till they are no more.

Psalm 59:12-13 (NKJV)


They fully intend to topple Him from His lofty place; they take delight in lies. With their mouths they bless, but in their hearts they curse.

Psalm 62:4 (NIV)

# TRUTH

But the king shall rejoice in God; every one that sweareth by Him shall glory: but the mouth of them that speak lies shall be stopped.

Psalm 63:11 (KJV)

Teach me Your way, O LORD, that I may walk in Your truth; unite my heart to fear Your name.

Psalm 86:11 (ESV)

No one who practices deceit will dwell in my house; no one who speaks falsely will stand in my presence.

Psalm 101:7 (NIV)

I have chosen the way of truth: Thy judgments have I laid before me.

Psalm 119:30 (KJV)

The sum of Your word is truth, and every one of Your righteous rules endures forever.

Psalm 119:160 (ESV)

# Victory

May we shout for joy over your salvation, and in the name of our God set up our banners! May the LORD fulfill all your petitions!

Psalm 20:5 (ESV)

By this I know that Thou favourest me, because mine enemy doth not triumph over me.

Psalm 41:11 (KJV)

For He has delivered me from all my troubles, and my eyes have looked in triumph on my foes.

Psalm 54:7 (NIV)

My God in His steadfast love will meet me; God will let me look in triumph on my enemies.

Psalm 59:10 (ESV)

Through God we shall do valiantly: for He it is that shall tread down our enemies.

Psalm 60:12 (KJV)

# VICTORY

He will have no fear of bad news; his heart is steadfast, trusting in the LORD. His heart is secure, he will have no fear; in the end he will look in triumph on his foes. He has scattered abroad his gifts to the poor, his righteousness endures forever; his horn will be lifted high in honor.

Psalm 112:7-9 (NIV)

The LORD is on my side; I will not fear. What can man do to me? The LORD is for me among those who help me; therefore I shall see my desire on those who hate me. The right hand of the LORD is exalted; the right hand of the LORD does valiantly.

Psalm 118:6-7, 16 (NKJV)

# WEALTH

Who, then, is the man that fears the LORD? He will instruct him in the way chosen for him. He will spend his days in prosperity, and his descendants will inherit the land.

Psalm 25:12-13 (NIV)

The young lions do lack, and suffer hunger: but they that seek the LORD shall not want any good thing.

Psalm 34:10 (KJV)

Be still before the LORD and wait patiently for Him; fret not yourself over the one who prospers in his way, over the man who carries out evil devices!

Psalm 37:7 (ESV)

A little that a righteous man hath is better than the riches of many wicked. The LORD knoweth the days of the upright: and their inheritance shall be for ever.

Psalm 37:16,18 (KJV)

# WEALTH

They that trust in their wealth, and boast themselves in the multitude of their riches; none of them can by any means redeem his brother, nor give to God a ransom for him: That he should still live for ever, and not see corruption. For he seeth that wise men die, likewise the fool and the brutish person perish, and leave their wealth to others.

Psalm 49:6-7, 9-10 (KJV)

Do not trust in oppression, nor vainly hope in robbery; if riches increase, do not set your heart on them.

Psalm 62:10 (NKJV)

Whom have I in heaven but You? And there is nothing on earth that I desire besides You.

Psalm 73:25 (ESV)

He provides food for those who fear Him; He remembers His covenant forever.

Psalm 111:5 (NIV)

# WISDOM

I will instruct you and teach you in the way you should go; I will counsel you and watch over you. Do not be like the horse or the mule, which have no understanding but must be controlled by bit and bridle.

Psalm 32:8-9 (NIV)

The mouth of the righteous speaks wisdom, and his tongue talks of justice. The law of his God is in his heart; none of his steps shall slide.

Psalm 37:30-31 (NKJV)

O LORD, make me know my end and what is the measure of my days; let me know how fleeting I am!

Psalm 39:4 (ESV)

My mouth will speak words of wisdom; the utterance from my heart will give understanding.

Psalm 49:3 (NIV)

# WISDOM

Man in his pomp yet without understanding is like the beasts that perish.

Psalm 49:20 (ESV)

Behold, Thou desirest truth in the inward parts: and in the hidden part Thou shalt make me to know wisdom.

Psalm 51:6 (KJV)

Teach us to number our days aright, that we may gain a heart of wisdom.

Psalm 90:12 (NIV)

He that chastiseth the heathen, shall not He correct? He that teacheth man knowledge, shall not He know?

Psalm 94:10 (KJV)

How many are Your works, O LORD! In wisdom You made them all; the earth is full of Your creatures.

Psalm 104:24 (NIV)

# WISDOM

Whoso is wise, and will observe these things, even they shall understand the lovingkindness of the LORD.

Psalm 107:43 (KJV)

The fear of the LORD is the beginning of wisdom; all those who practice it have a good understanding. His praise endures forever!

Psalm 111:10 (ESV)

Give me understanding, and I shall keep Your law; I shall observe it with my whole heart.

Psalm 119:34 (NKJV)

The unfolding of Your words gives light; it gives understanding to the simple.

Psalm 119:130 (NIV)

The righteousness of Your testimonies is everlasting; give me understanding, and I shall live.

Psalm 119:144 (NKJV)

*Your word*

is a *lamp* for my feet,

a *light* on my path.

Psalm 119:105